EXTREME SKIING

by John E. Schindler

GARETH**STEVENS**
PUBLISHING
A WRC Media Company

Please visit our web site at: www.garethstevens.com
For a free color catalog describing Gareth Stevens Publishing's
list of high-quality books and multimedia programs,
call 1-800-542-2595 (USA) or 1-800-387-3178 (Canada).
Gareth Stevens Publishing's fax: (414) 332-3567.

Library of Congress Cataloging-in-Publication Data available upon request from publisher.
Fax (414) 336-0157 for the attention of the Publishing Records Department.

ISBN 0-8368-4539-0 (lib. bdg.)
ISBN 0-8368-4546-3 (softcover)

First published in 2005 by
Gareth Stevens Publishing
A WRC Media Company
330 West Olive Street, Suite 100
Milwaukee, WI 53212 USA

Text: John E. Schindler
Cover design and page layout: Tammy West
Series editor: Carol Ryback
Photo research: Diane Laska-Swanke

Photo credits: Cover © Ken Levine/WireImage.com; pp. 5, 15 © Christian Perret/Jump;
pp. 7, 13, 17, 19 © Howie Garber/Wanderlust Images; p. 9 © www.guntermarx-stockphotos.com;
p. 11 © Alden Pellet/R. Clarkson & Assoc./WireImage.com; p. 21 © Christian Pondella.com,
H2O Heli Guides of Alaska

Printed in the United States of America

1 2 3 4 5 6 7 8 9 09 08 07 06 05

Cover: Extreme skiers practice long and hard to do amazing tricks, such as this complete flip in the air, while on skis.

TABLE OF CONTENTS

Words that appear in the glossary are printed in **boldface** type the first time they occur in the text.

EXTREME FUN

Snow skis were not invented for fun. People first used them for travel. Snow skiing for fun started in the last one hundred years or so.

In the 1980s, some daring skiers thought of new, exciting, and wild ways to ski. They invented a group of winter ski sports called extreme skiing.

Extreme skiers do flips and tricks off **ski jumps**. They ski down very steep hills. Some ride in helicopters to the tops of mountains and ski down. Others **skydive** onto mountaintops wearing skis.

No matter how they get up to the top, extreme skiers find wild ways to get to the bottom!

An extreme skier takes a daring leap off a steep mountain. Sometimes skiers cannot see where they will land until they are in the air!

SKI EARLY, SKI OFTEN

Extreme skiers usually learn to ski when they are kids. They go skiing a lot. Even when they are very young, they try to ski down almost any hill.

Extreme skiers use different skis for different kinds of skiing. Long skis make skiers go faster. Short skis help skiers turn easily. **Telemark** skis let skiers move more freely than other types of skis.

All skiers wear special ski boots. Ski bindings hold the boots to the skis. When the skier falls, the bindings loosen. The boots fall out of the skis.

Most skiers use ski poles to help make turns.

A skier on telemark skis pulls his legs close to his body to jump into the air.

CATCHING BIG AIR

Skiers use ski jumps to make long jumps. They hope to land far past the end of the jump. Extreme ski jumpers use ski jumps to do spins, flips, and twists. Tricks done in the air are called **aerials**.

A ski jump built for aerials ends with a steep snow lip, or edge, called a kicker. The kicker helps skiers get high into the air. Skiers who do tricks high in the air are called **aerialists**.

The best aerialists might go 50 feet (15 meters) high or higher. They do many backflips, twists, and spins before landing.

An aerialist does a perfect backflip. She took off from the left ski jump to get high in the air.

FASTEST SPORT ON EARTH?

Skiing down a hill as fast as possible is called speed skiing. It is the fastest sport on Earth without a motor. Speed skiers can reach speeds of more than 150 miles (241 kilometers) per hour!

Speed skiing skis are very long and wide. All speed skiers wear helmets. Most speed skiers also wear tight, smooth suits coated with a thin layer of rubber or plastic. The helmets and smooth suits help them go down the hill faster.

Skiing downhill at these high speeds is very dangerous. Some skiers wear special padding so they do not get hurt.

A speed skier needs special safety gear, such as a helmet, a sleek wind suit, and lower-leg pads.

GETTING AWAY FROM IT ALL

Extreme skiers sometimes ski the **backcountry**. The backcountry is different from the regular downhill skiing places. It does not have **chairlifts**. Backcountry skiers climb to the top carrying their skis. They must be careful to stay safe.

Other backcountry skiers travel for long distances. They wear long telemark skis. The bindings on telemark skis let skiers lift their heels. Skiers wearing telemark skis can go uphill or downhill. These long skis also make skiing on flat land easy.

Smart backcountry skiers of all types always tell someone where they are going.

A backcountry skier enjoys skiing through the trees. Snow is often very deep in the backcountry.

TO HELI-SKI AND BACK

What is a good way to get to the extremely high, backcountry mountaintops faster? Hop in a helicopter! Riding a helicopter to reach the top of a mountain so you can ski down is called **heli-skiing**.

Once the helicopter lands, you jump out onto the mountain. You and your friends put on your skis and blast down the slopes. Now you are skiing where no one has skied before.

You should only go heli-skiing if you are a very good extreme skier. Skiing down steep mountains is very dangerous. If you fall, you could get hurt really badly.

Seven extreme skiers leave trails in fresh snow after a helicopter ride to the mountaintop.

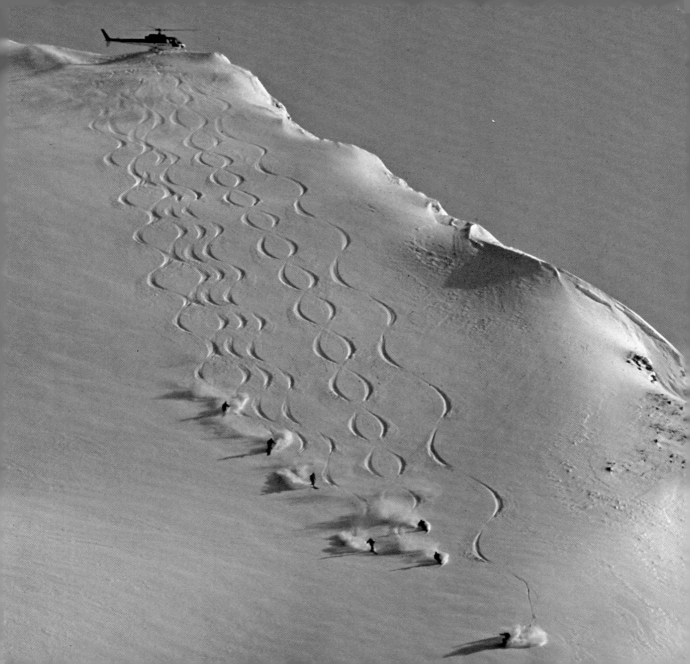

SNOW SAFETY RULES

Extreme skiing is much safer when skiers are well prepared. Mountain air is very dry. All skiers need to drink lots of water.

Backcountry skiers often carry water and a small shovel to dig a snow shelter if the weather turns bad.

Skiers can sometimes cause an **avalanche**. An avalanche is a pile of snow that breaks loose near a mountaintop. As it falls, it knocks even more snow down the mountain.

All extreme skiers carry a radio that gives off a signal. The signal helps find skiers who might be buried by an avalanche.

This backcountry skier carries a backpack loaded with a radio, extra clothing, and water.

BLADES AND BIKES

Some extreme skiers, called **blade runners**, like to skydive to their favorite ski places. Blade runners get down close to the snow, but they do not land. They use their parachutes to stay in the air. They "ski" without touching the snow!

Blade runners follow a set of poles down the mountain. Long skinny flags, called blades, hang sideways from the poles.

Extreme skiers wearing short skis might ride bikes down mountains. Ski bikes have skis instead of wheels. Extreme skiers sit on ski bikes and ride to the bottom.

Maybe you will invent a new extreme skiing sport!

Can you think of a name for this extreme sport? Would you like to do this someday? Maybe you will!

EXTREME CHAMPIONS

Extreme skiers work out hard to build strong muscles. They do bending and stretching exercises.

Some aerialist extreme skiers use **trampolines** to practice doing aerials. They use safety ropes hooked to their waists. Ropes keep them from falling off the trampolines.

Other extreme ski jumpers practice their flips and turns over water. If they fall, they just get wet.

Heli-skiers practice on extreme slopes around the globe. They might enter the World Extreme Ski Championships for heli-skiing in Valdez, Alaska.

Can you become an extreme skiing champion? Yes — now get out there and ski!

A heli-skier zooms down Hogback Mountain in Valdez, Alaska, creating a cloud of snow around himself.

MORE TO READ AND VIEW

Books (Nonfiction) *Downhill Skiing: A Level Two Reader. Wonder Books Level-2 Sports.* Cynthia Fitterer Klingel

Extreme Downhill Skiing Moves. Behind the Moves (series). Mary Firestone. (Capstone High-Interest Books)

Skiing. Larry Dane Brimner. (Children's Press)

Skiing. Radical Sports (series). Paul Mason. (Heinemann)

Skiing In Action. Sports in Action (series). John Crossingham. (Crabtree)

Skiing Is for Me. The Sports for Me Books (series). Annette Jo Chappell (Lerner)

Books (Fiction) *I Can Ski. Rookie Readers* (series). Melanie Davis Jones. (Children's Press)

Mutley Goes Skiing. Gene Alba. (Heian International)

DVDs and Videos *Extreme Winter (2000).* (E-Realbiz.com)

Warren Miller's Extreme Skiing 3. (Columbia/Tristar Studios)

22

WEB SITES

Web sites change frequently, but the following web sites should last awhile. You can also search Google (*www.google.com*) or Yahooligans! (*www.yahooligans.com*) for more information about extreme skiing. Some keywords to help your search include: *chutes, cliff jumping, couloirs, freeskiing, heli-skiing, moguls, off-piste terrain, ski resorts for kids, tree skiing*.

www.ehow.com/list_1076.html
Scroll down to "skiing" for answers to skiing questions. Includes tips on choosing gear, what to eat before you go skiing, and how to do tricks on skis.

jacksonhole.snowmonsters.com/ index.cfm?fuseaction=kidsclub. home
Check out Jackson Hole Ski Resort's kids' page. Follow links to the kids' club, snow games, skiing tips, and more.

www.ski-bike.org/
Click "gallery" to see pictures of people on ski bikes. Other links tell the history of ski biking, where to do it, and how to get started.

yahooligans.yahoo.com/games_ popup.php?g=arcade_sk2_skigame
Play online games, such as skiing downhill, cross-country, or slalom.

GLOSSARY

You can find these words on the pages listed. Reading a word in a sentence helps you understand it even better.

aerialist — a skier who does tricks in the air. 8, 20

aerials — ski tricks done in the air. 8, 20

avalanche — a very large, heavy pile of snow sliding down a mountain. 16

backcountry — a place that is not part of the regular skiing land. 12, 14, 16

blade runners — skiers who skydive onto ski hills and then ski to the bottoms of the hills between tall flags called blades. 18

chairlifts — motorized seats on a set of cables that go to the top of a mountain. 12

heli-skiing — using a helicopter to take you to where you are going to ski. 14, 20

ski biking — riding a bicycle that has skis instead of wheels down a ski hill. 18

ski jumps — long high ramps used for ski jumping. 4, 8

skydive — to jump from an airplane and float down using a parachute. 4, 18

telemark — a ski that lets skiers move their heels. It also means using those skis. 6, 12

trampoline — a sheet of thick fabric for jumping on that is held up by springs. 20

INDEX